Alfie

ᴛʜᴇ SCHOOLBOY ENTREPRENEUR

BOOK FOUR

Alfie
and the
Toy Hunter

Mark Hibbitts

Illustrated by Anna Bishop

bookshaker

First Published in Great Britain 2015 by
www.BookShaker.com

© Copyright Mark Hibbitts
Illustrations by Anna Bishop

"Very narrow areas of expertise can be very productive. Develop your own profile. Develop your own niche."
Leigh Steinberg

Contents

An Idea

"Alfie Potts was an entrepreneur."

Unlike most twelve year old boys, Alfie was learning how to get rich…

…but today he was sitting in front of the telly.

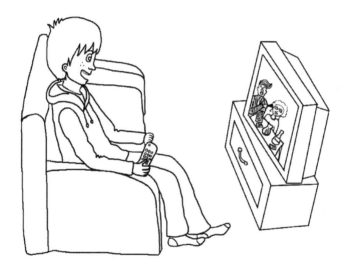

Alfie didn't watch much TV because he felt it was a waste of his time, but he'd noticed this programme had 'cash' in the title and he was looking for new ideas.

The programme was about some people who were clearing all the junk out of their house, pricing it up, and selling it at a local car boot sale. And, over the course of the 30 minute show, the 'junk' they'd found in their gardens, attics, cupboards, and garages had sold for several hundred pounds!

Alfie was excited.

"Daaaad!" shouted Alfie. "Have you and mum got any stuff lying around the house that you want to get rid of?"

"Hmmm, I don't know Alfie," said Dad, thoughtfully. "Like what?"

"Like anything," replied Alfie. "I'm gonna do a car boot sale!"

"That sounds like a good idea son," said Dad. "One man's junk is another man's treasure, so they say! I'm sure we can find a few things for you… and I'll bet if you look through your toys you'll find a lot of stuff you don't use too."

"Aw, Dad," said Alfie, frowning. "I don't want to sell *my* stuff. I still play with it all."

"Ha ha," laughed Dad. "I thought you might say that! And I'm also certain that's not totally true. I think it's time I taught you about *the vacuum law of prosperity* son."

"The what?" said Alfie, grinning at his Dad.

"The vacuum law of prosperity Alfie. It's very simple but very important if you want to have some nice new things in your life. Simply put, nature doesn't like a vacuum and will always fill it as soon as it can. Therefore, if you want some new stuff, get rid of some old stuff and create a vacuum. It won't be long before the universe fills it with something else. Something better."

"As simple as that?" questioned Alfie.

"Yes son, as simple as that–Hey! Where are you running off to now?"

"Up to my room Dad," shouted Alfie from the stairs. "I've just thought of a few things I haven't played with for a while."

***

Alfie Potts was a quick learner…

Alfie spent the next few days sorting out all his old toys, clothes, and anything else he could get his hands on that wasn't totally worthless, and separating them into piles for sale. There was also a lot of stuff his mum and dad had given him, and he sorted that out too.

Then they all got together to decide on prices for the items Alfie would be selling. Dad told Alfie that most people will try to knock the prices down as much as they can, so they priced them all a little higher to leave room for the hagglers[1].

There were also a few other things they weren't really sure about, so they decided that on the day of the sale, Alfie should use his entrepreneurial judgement when pricing them up.

By Friday evening the car was packed, and Alfie was ready for Saturday's sale...

---

[1] Hagglers: People who argue over price to try and get a bargain (you should do this!)

A New Friend

Alfie and his Dad were up very early the next morning, and by 7 am they were parked in the middle of a large field. Even at that time of day there were lots of people there, and Alfie was shocked to find people coming up to their car and trying to rummage though their stuff before they'd even unpacked.

"Hey!" he exclaimed to one particularly rude man. "Hold on! We're not ready yet!" The man scowled, then shrugged his shoulders and moved onto the next car.

"There was a good business lesson for you there Alfie," said dad, laughing. "You can generate a lot of excitement when something new comes on to the market!"

Alfie looked at his dad and grinned, and they continued with their unpacking.

By half past seven they had their tables set up and all their stuff was out on display for sale.

People milled round Alfie's table, picking up toys and books, looking at them, testing them to see if they worked and, of course, offering him money for them!

Alfie loved it. And with so much stuff to sell it wasn't long before he had nearly fifty pounds in his pocket!

"This is great Dad," he said with a smile. "I'm getting rid of loads of stuff!"

"You're doing well," replied Dad. "Alfie you'll be ok here for a minute won't you son? I'm just popping over to that van to get a cup of tea, is there anything you want?"

"Yeah, I'll be fine Dad, and I'll have an apple juice if they've got one. Thanks."

Alfie's Dad went off to get their drinks, and Alfie looked around the field. The sun was shining and there were still plenty of people driving in, even though it was nearly ten o'clock.

"I wonder how much money I'll take today," thought Alfie to himself. "And what am I going to do with it…"

Suddenly a voice jolted him out of his daydream…

"Excuse me! How much do you want for this car?"

Alfie looked round quickly to see a girl of about his own age holding up a small box with a gold car in it. She'd found it in one of his boxes.

"Sorry to wake you up!" she said to him with a grin.

The girl was extremely pretty and Alfie felt himself blushing.

"Er… that's alright," he replied. "Um… you can have that one for three quid."

"Make it two-fifty and you've got a deal," replied the girl, looking him straight in the eye.

"Yeah ok," said Alfie, taking the money and putting it into his pocket.

"Thanks. See you around then," said the smiling girl, giving Alfie a little wave as she walked off.

"Er… yeah… bye then," muttered Alfie, wondering why he felt a bit strange.

"Here's your juice son," said Dad as he returned with the drinks. "What's been happening?"

"Nothing really," said Alfie, distractedly. "Sold another car, that's all."

"That's good then. We still have a few hours to go, and you won't be taking much stuff back home with you at this rate."

Another hour quickly passed, and Alfie sold even more of his and his parents' stuff until only a few things remained.

"Why don't you take a little break Alfie?" said his Dad. "You've worked really hard. Have a look around and see if there's anything interesting you want to buy."

"Great idea Dad!" said Alfie enthusiastically. "Hold the fort for me and I'll be back in a bit."

Alfie spent ten minutes wandering round the field looking at all the stuff that was left on the 'car booters' tables, but it seemed like most of the good stuff had gone early.

Then he stopped suddenly and caught his breath.

There was the girl he'd seen earlier. She was standing behind one of the tables, and it looked like she was selling his car to someone else!

But he wasn't paying her with coins. He was paying her with notes!

LOTS OF NOTES!!!

Alfie sneaked to the side of her table without being seen, and hid behind a clothes rail.

"Thank you so much! I've been looking for this model for years," gushed the man excitedly. "Here's your fifty pounds. That's a good price for an original[2] one like this."

"It is," he heard the girl say. "So, we're both happy then? You know if it still had everything with it you'd have had to pay a lot more than that?"

"Oh yes, I know," said the man.

Alfie couldn't believe his ears. The man had given her FIFTY POUNDS!

He'd sold it to her earlier for two pounds fifty… *and* she'd had the cheek to knock him down from three quid!

Once the man had left Alfie stepped out from behind the clothes rail.

"Hey! That was my car wasn't it!" he said to the girl.

"Yes." replied the girl without a trace of guilt. "At least it was until you sold it to *me!*"

---

[2] Original: One of the first ones made. Not a later copy.

"But I didn't know it was worth all that," said Alfie, "and you obviously did. Do you think that was fair of you?"

"That depends on how you look at it," said the girl. "I guess I could have told you what it was really worth when I saw it. Perhaps that would have been a nice thing to do. But then what would be the point of all the hours of research I put in to get my specialist knowledge needed to hunt collectible[3] toys? I do it to make money after all."

Alfie thought back to an earlier lesson his Dad had taught him about value to the marketplace. This girl had obviously invested lots of time and effort to make herself more valuable, so who was he to deny her the chance to profit from that knowledge.

"Yes, you're right," he said. "I would have done the same thing. It's not really the money that's bothering me, it's the fact that I'm selling things and I haven't done my homework to

---

[3] Collectible: An item valued and sought after by collectors.

find out what they're really worth. I wonder how many other things I've priced wrongly today?"

"None," said the girl. "I had a good look at your stuff when you were unpacking it this morning and the car was the only collectible thing there. That was an original James Bond Aston Martin DB5! I just had to pick my moment to come and buy it."

Alfie laughed. "You're really sneaky, but I have to admit, you know your stuff."

The girl laughed too and flashed that smile again. "Tracey Bryan," she said holding out her hand. "And you're Alfie Potts aren't you?"

"Yes," said Alfie, shaking her hand, "How did you know that?"

"Aha!" she said, grinning. "I'm starting at your school soon, and my cousin has told me about your business ventures. That's why I was so surprised that you didn't know the value of that car."

"Humph," grunted Alfie, feeling a bit dumb, but flattered nonetheless. "Well, I guess it's nice to be recognised! Have you lived here long?"

"No," said Tracey, grinning. "I only moved here last month. I live down the road there on Leverage Lane."

"Wow, that's not far away from Fortune Street where I live," said Alfie. "Will you come round one day and teach me about collectibles. I've obviously got a lot to learn in that department."

"I'd love to," said Tracey, passing Alfie a piece of paper and a pen. "Here… write down my name and address… you'll probably do it faster than me."

"Why do you think that?" said Alfie, puzzled.

"Because I have dyslexia[4]," said Tracey,

"Oh, ok," said Alfie, puzzled.

It was obvious to Tracey that Alfie didn't know what 'dyslexia' meant, and she

---

[4] Dyslexia: A reading/writing difficulty in a child or adult who otherwise has good intelligence, strong motivation and adequate schooling (basic definition).

giggled… "It means I find reading and writing a bit… shall we say… challenging… so I don't always do great in class. But it's not a big deal because I already know what I'm going to do when I grow up."

She told him her address and telephone number and said, "Well, I'd better get on now because it's time to pack up. No hard feelings then?"

"No… I guess not," replied Alfie, tucking the piece of paper into his jeans pocket. "See you again soon!"

"Yes you will," Tracey replied with another smile, and she started packing away what was left of her stock.

As Alfie turned away to walk back to his table he was grinning all over his face.

The Niche Market

On the way home Alfie told his Dad about Tracey and the car, and he was surprised when his Dad started laughing.

"It's not funny Dad! I could have had another fifty quid on top of this," he said angrily as he waved the wad of notes in the air.

Alfie's Dad was still chuckling when he said, "I'm afraid there will be times Alfie, just like today, where you won't come out on top. What's more important is that you learn from them and use the knowledge you gain to your advantage. You'll always learn more from losing than you will from winning son, and entrepreneurs are not afraid of making mistakes."

"Really Dad?" said Alfie

"Really son," he replied. "Thomas Edison, the man who invented the incandescent[5] light bulb, actually failed 10,000 times before he got it right."

"10,000 times?" exclaimed Alfie. "That's amazing!"

"Yes son. And at the time he said, 'I haven't failed. I've just found 10,000 ways that don't work.' Now that's an entrepreneurial attitude[6]! Most people give up after the first failure. Some may try again. But the really successful people out there just keep on trying until they find something that works… Anyhow, what did you learn from today?"

"Er… well I guess I learned that some things can be worth a lot more than you

---

[5] Incandescent: Containing a filament that glows white-hot when heated by a current passed through it.

[6] Attitude: A way of thinking that is reflected in a person's behaviour.

think, and that if I'm going to sell stuff I should make sure I know what it is I'm selling or I may lose out," replied Alfie.

"That's certainly true," said Dad, nodding his head as he drove home. "Especially if you work in a niche market[7] like Tracey does."

"A niche market?" replied Alfie. "What's that?"

"Well, if you have a niche market son, it means you operate in a reasonably small and specialist, but usually quite profitable marketplace, just like Tracey does with toys. She must be quite a smart cookie Alfie. When are we going to meet her?"

"Soon," said Alfie. Then he asked, "Dad, what's 'dyslexic'?

"Well basically it means you can have some difficulty learning to read, write, and spell," said Dad. "But there's a bit more to it

---

[7] Niche: A small, specialist, and usually profitable marketplace. People who operate in niche markets are often experts in their trade.

than that and some people have dyslexia more severely than others. Why do you ask son?"

"Tracey's dyslexic," said Alfie, "She told me earlier."

"Oh, I see," replied Dad. "Well I can't see that holding her back unless she lets it Alfie. Some of the most famous entrepreneurs in the world are dyslexic. Take Sir Richard Branson for example and Theo Paphitis from Dragons' Den on the TV. They are both dyslexic and look at what they've accomplished!"

"Wow, that's great Dad. I think I'll give her a call tomorrow," said Alfie. "I want her to teach me everything she knows about toy hunting!"

Over the next few weeks Alfie and Tracey spent a lot of time together, each of them enjoying the ambition and sense of purpose they saw in the other. They studied all the magazines and books on rare and collectible toys that Tracey owned, and they Googled all the articles they could find about toys that had sold for lots of money around the world.

Alfie learned fast, and the pair constantly tested each other on their knowledge. Both had a strong desire to learn and grow, and not spend all their time watching TV and playing games like a lot of the other children they knew. They spent the odd day out at local car boot sales and antique fairs, and it wasn't long before they started picking up a few bargains and selling them for a profit on ebay[8] and in collectors' magazines.

This just whetted their appetite for more.

<hr />

[8] www.ebay.com: A popular internet auction website.

"I think Tracey and I could make some real money at this Dad," said Alfie one afternoon after she'd gone home to finish her homework.

"You probably could son," replied Dad. "Maybe the two of you should form a proper joint venture[9]."

"A joint venture? What's one of those?" asked Alfie.

"Well it means that you form a temporary partnership to carry out a particular project. In this case a toy business." said Dad. "You can share the investment[10] and your knowledge, and then you can split the profits that you make… if and when you make them of course!"

"Yeah that sounds like a plan Dad!" replied Alfie enthusiastically. "We could do

---

[9] Joint Venture: An agreement or partnership between two or more parties to undertake a business activity together.

[10] Investment: The process of putting money into a business or venture with an expectation of future profit.

that. I think Tracey would be up for it, I'll ask her tomorrow."

Alfie was right. The next day he told Tracey what Dad had suggested and she agreed that a joint venture was a great idea.

They decided to invest £100 each of their own money, and they developed a business plan[11] where they would visit the local collectors' fairs, auctions, and car boot sales, open a proper ebay shop, advertise for old toys in the local free magazines, and run a real profit and loss account[12] so they could accurately measure how their business was doing.

It was fun! Of course there were times when there was nothing to be found at the car boots, and there were times when things sold at auction for more than they were willing to pay, but they usually managed to find

---

[11] Business Plan: A written document which describes the business, its objectives, its strategies, the market in which it operates and its financial forecasts.

[12] Profit and Loss Account: A financial statement showing net profit or loss in a given period.

something that would later give them a profit. Plus all the time Alfie's knowledge of toys, especially cars, was getting better until he knew as much as Tracey!

One day when they were looking at the local 'ad trader' magazine Alfie pointed and said, "Look Tracey! There's a three day collectors' fair in a fortnight over at The Showground. I'll ask Dad to take us. This is a big one, and it's only on once a year!"

"Wow, that would be great," replied Tracey, her heart already starting to beat faster thinking of all the old toys they would see, and, even more importantly, what treasures they might unearth.

When Dad looked in his diary and said he could take them to the first day, they started to plan their strategy.

"I think we need to take all the money we have to this one," said Alfie. "At a fair this size there's no telling what we may find!"

"I agree with you," said Tracey. "We could stock up for the next few months at this one, and I'd hate to see something and not have the cash to buy it. We've got just over £250 at the moment, so let's hope that's enough."

The next 3 weeks seemed to go by so slowly and Alfie and Tracey impatiently counted the days. Finally it was the day before the fair and they couldn't wait!

"We'll pick you up really early tomorrow Tracey. About 6 am. Is that ok?" said Alfie excitedly.

"Yes! As early as you like," replied Tracey, laughing. "I doubt if I'll be getting much sleep tonight. I'm far too excited for that!"

The Find

The next morning Alfie was up and dressed early and waiting at the door for Dad to get his coat on.

"Come on Dad," he said. "We don't want to be late and miss anything."

"I'm coming son," said Dad a little groggily. "Be patient. It's only half past five!"

Tracey was waiting by the front door when they got there, and when she saw them she came running down the path and jumped into the back of Alfie's dad's car.

"I thought you'd never get here!" she exclaimed.

Alfie laughed, "I know! Dad isn't at his best in the morning!"

Dad looked across at Alfie. "A very wise man named Ralph Waldo Emerson once said that 'nothing great was ever achieved without enthusiasm.' If he was right then you two will have nothing to worry about!" he said with a smile.

It only took 20 minutes to get to The Showground. When they arrived they walked right into the hustle and bustle of people carrying boxes full of collectibles and antiques[13], and stalls being set up.

---

[13] Antique: A collectible object such as a piece of furniture or work of art that has a high value because of its considerable age

"I love it here already!" said Alfie. "I just know we're going to have a good day."

"I know what you mean." replied Tracey "What a fantastic atmosphere. Where shall we start?"

"Well I know where I'm starting," said Alfie's Dad with a grin.

"Where?" asked both the children eagerly.

"Over there at the coffee stall," laughed Dad. "I'm still not awake yet! You two carry on. You know where I'll be if you need me."

"Very funny Dad," said Alfie. Then he pointed and said, "Look Tracey! Over there… that seems to be where most of the toys are."

"I see them," said Tracey, and they both scampered off to where Alfie had been pointing.

There were lots and lots of stalls, and the children spent ages rummaging through boxes of cars, trucks, trains, boats, and even dolls (Tracey liked dolls, and said that some were quite valuable, but Alfie wasn't convinced), but it was all to no avail. After two long hours they hadn't found one thing that could have been considered a bargain.

"No luck yet?" asked Dad when they came back to him empty handed for the third time. "Maybe it's not going to be your day today after all."

"Well it's not looking good so far Dad, but it's still early yet," answered Alfie, "and I'm certainly not giving up so soon."

"No, me neither!" said Tracey. There are still some stalls we haven't looked at."

But things didn't improve, and by lunchtime the two children were starting to look a bit despondent.

"We've done all the toy stalls now Dad and we've found nothing," said Alfie unhappily as they sat round the table eating their sandwiches.

"That's a real shame," said Dad. "There will always be days when things don't go right for you. It's the same for everyone son, and that's just the way it is. But it's not the things going wrong… It's how you react to the things going wrong that's important."

"How do you mean Mr Potts?" said Tracey, who was listening intently.

"I mean, when something doesn't go your way, you can get cross, say it's not fair, and blame other people," said Alfie's Dad, smiling. "Or you can take responsibility and say ok that didn't work, so how can I do it better next time? That's the attitude of a successful person Tracey."

"Yes, I guess it is," she replied, starting to look a little brighter.

Then they both turned to look at Alfie who had gone a bit quiet. He was sitting there with his mouth wide open, looking very intently at one of the stalls.

"What's wrong Alfie?" said Tracey. "What on earth are you looking at?"

Alfie put his finger to his lips as if to say 'Shhh' then he whispered, "Over there… on that table… the truck… it can't be… can it?"

He was pointing to an old yellow toy dump truck that a man was placing on a table with a bunch of other toys. It took a little while, but when Tracey finally saw the object Alfie was talking about, her jaw dropped and her eyes opened wide like saucers.

"No!" she said in amazement. "It's not possible… is it? How on earth did we miss that?"

"He's only just got it out, that's how," gasped Alfie.

"What have you seen?" said Alfie's Dad, who was starting to get a bit worried about the children's strange behaviour.

"We're not quite sure yet," replied Alfie. "But it looks very much like a Lesney Prototype, doesn't it Tracey? The only thing is Dad… there shouldn't be any of them left!"

Tracey nodded in agreement.

Alfie said, "Stay here dad, we'll be back in a minute," and the two of them started walking hurriedly towards the stall.

When they got there Alfie reached out and picked up the truck. As he looked at it he had to really concentrate to stop his hands from shaking. He turned it over in his hands then passed it over to Tracey.

"I think it is," she whispered through her teeth.

"Me too," Alfie whispered back. "But there's no price on it."

"No, I noticed that," Tracey replied. "I'll ask the man behind the stall how much he wants for it."

"Well do it quietly," said Alfie looking around at all the people. "We don't want anyone else to see this, do we?"

Tracey took the truck to the grumpy looking trader who was sitting at the back of his stall drinking a cup of tea.

"Excuse me," she said with her sweetest smile. "How much is this old truck?"

"Hmmm, I'm not sure about that." grunted the man. "I picked it up in a house clearance[14] a while back. Toys aren't really my strong point, but I think it's pretty old and rare. I reckon I'd need a hundred quid for that one."

"Wow! A hundred pounds? That's a lot of money for this old thing," said Tracey with a frown.

"Maybe it is, but maybe it isn't," answered the man. "It's up to you isn't it? I'm going to take it over to one of the toy car experts when I've finished this tea and see what they make of it..."

"Well hang on a minute. I haven't said I didn't want it," said Tracey indignantly. "I just said that it seemed a bit expensive. Let me have a word with my friend."

---

[14] House Clearance: Buying and taking away the entire contents of a property in one go.

She took the truck and turned around to face Alfie. "He doesn't have a clue what it could be Alfie! He reminds me of you a month ago," she said with a chuckle.

"Oh, stop it," said Alfie with a wry grin. "Things have changed since then. How much did he want for it?"

"He said a hundred pounds, but we can probably knock him down a bit. We'll have to be quick though because he wants to take it over to the toy car specialists. One of them will definitely know what it's worth!" whispered Tracey.

"Yes they will," said Alfie thoughtfully. "But what if we're wrong and it's not what we think it is. That means we'll be a hundred pounds out of pocket, and that's a lot of money."

"You're right, it is," replied Tracey. "What shall we do?"

They looked at the yellow truck over and over again, and the more they looked the more doubts started creeping in to their minds. They'd seen pictures of a truck just like this many times in their magazines and books, and this one looked identical, but was it really possible? Out of the six that were made there was supposed to be only one left in existence, and that had been sold to a collector at auction last year.

This one just shouldn't be here…

"Well do you want it or not?" said the impatient stall holder, tipping the last of his tea down his throat. "If not, give it here. I'm taking it over to the experts."

"Quick Alfie," said Tracey. "What are we going to do? I think it's the real thing, do you?"

Alfie stood paralysed for a moment as negative thoughts kept running through his head.

What if it's not what we think it is?
What if we waste our money?
What if it's a fake?
What if…? What if…?

Then the words his Dad had said to him on the way home from car boot sale popped into his head… *Entrepreneurs are not afraid of making mistakes."*

Don't be afraid of making a mistake thought Alfie to himself. We've done our homework and we know our niche inside out. I reckon that between us Tracey and I know as much about collectible toys as anyone and we both think this feels right. Go on, make him an offer.

"I'll give you fifty quid for it!" said Alfie to the man. "I like it but I don't like it that much!"

"Your boyfriend drives a hard bargain!" said the man to Tracey, making her blush. "But I want a bit more than that, how about eighty?"

"Well I can go to seventy five I suppose" said Alfie, "But that's it… and I'm *not* her boyfriend, we're just mates!" he added quickly.

The man grinned. "Oh alright, it'll save me the bother of taking it over to the experts and making a fool of myself."

He took Alfie's cash and gave them a bag to put the truck in. Alfie and Tracey stuffed the truck into the bag, waited for their receipt[15] and then they rushed back to see Dad.

"That was a long minute!" said Alfie's Dad, looking at his watch. "I've been watching you for ages. You bought it then? How much did it cost you?"

---

[15] A written acknowledgment that a specified sum of money has been received in exchange for goods or services.

"Seventy Five pounds Dad," replied Alfie. "And, if it's what we think it is, we've got the deal of a lifetime!"

"Oh yes we have!" laughed Tracey happily.

"Let's hope it is then," said Dad. "Shall we go home now?"

"Yes!" shouted both children at once. They had more research[16] to do!

---

[16] An attempt to find out new information in a systematic and sometimes scientific manner.

The Auction

"Dad you'd better come and look at this," said Alfie, the next afternoon. "We've spent all day researching and we're pretty sure this is the real thing."

"Wow! I think you're right," said Dad after he'd examined all their information. "But if we're going to know for sure I'd better make a quick phone call."

He took out his phone and dialled a number… "Hello," he said into the phone. "I'd like to bring in something for a valuation[17] as soon as possible… a toy truck… yes I think it's extremely rare… tomorrow afternoon? Yes that'll be fine… it's Mr Potts… thank you very much… see you then."

---

[17] An estimation of something's worth carried out by a professional expert.

"Who was that Dad?" asked Alfie with a puzzled look on his face.

"That was Sotheby's, the world famous auction[18] house," replied his Dad. "All will be revealed tomorrow afternoon. I've booked it in for a valuation."

"Can we all go?" said Tracey.

"Of course we can," said Dad. "It's your truck after all."

---

[18] Auction: A sale in which goods or property are sold to the highest bidder.

"Wicked!" said the children.

The next day Alfie's Dad drove Alfie and Tracey to London for their appointment at Sotheby's. Both children were very excited, and they kept the truck safely between them on the back seat in a cardboard box padded with bubble wrap.

When they'd parked they all walked into the reception area and Dad spoke to the lady at the desk.

"Hello," he said. "We've brought something in to be valued. I made an appointment yesterday."

"Ah yes, I remember. Mr Potts isn't it?" said the lady, picking up the telephone on her desk. "Mr Potts is here," she said into the receiver. Then she turned back to Alfie's Dad. "Our toy expert will be down to see you in a few minutes Mr Potts. Please take a seat over there."

A short while later a man in a suit and a bowtie came down the corridor, stopped, and shook all their hands. "So," he said, smiling, "what do you have to show me?"

A nervous Alfie opened the box with trembling hands and took out the package. He placed it on the chair and quickly pulled the bubble wrap from the outside. Then he held it out for the toy expert to see.

"No! I don't believe it... it can't be... it's impossible..." said the expert, turning the truck over and over in his hands. "Quick, follow me," he said. He turned and walked up the corridor then he turned right and entered another room.

Alfie, Tracey and Dad had to almost run to keep up with him. The toy expert pulled down a book from the big bookcase that covered one whole wall and he frantically flicked through the pages. Then he pulled out a large magnifying glass and went over the truck in minute detail, stopping every few seconds to consult the open book.

Alfie, Tracey and Dad stood there looking at each other nervously, and wondering when the man was going to say something.

At last he stopped what he was doing and looked at them.

"Have you any idea what this is?" he asked Alfie.

"Well, we think it's a 1955 Matchbox Lesney dumper truck prototype," replied Alfie. "But we thought there weren't any left."

"Yes," said the expert, giving Alfie and Tracey a respectful look. "You're right. There were only six made, and the only one thought to be left was sold at auction last year. I saw that one and I've checked this one and, although it seems impossible, they are absolutely identical. I really can't believe it, but this is definitely the genuine article. You've found another!"

"YES!" shouted the children. "We knew it!"

"Well done both of you," said Alfie's Dad. "I knew all that studying would pay off!"

"It certainly has," said the expert. "Now, the real question is do you want to sell it? We have a specialist toy auction coming up next week, and this would be the icing on the cake for all our collectors. There will be *so* much interest… and I suppose you know what the last one sold for?"

"Yes, we know," replied Tracey with a big smile. "And yes, we want to sell it, don't we Alfie?"

"Oh yes we do!" said an elated Alfie Potts.

***

The Auction at Sotheby's was packed. People had come from far and wide when the news got out about the truck. Even the newspapers were there to see what price it made, and Tracey's mum and dad had come along with Alfie's to share in the excitement.

They all sat at the back of the auction room and watched as the other lots got sold.

As the truck was the star of the show Sotheby's had listed it last, and as it got closer they could feel the tension building in the room. The toy expert came over and stood next to them.

"Here we go," he whispered with a smile.

"Ok," started the auctioneer. "This is the moment you've all been waiting for. We are down to the very last lot. It's a long lost piece that has just come to light, and we are thrilled to have it here to auction off to the highest bidder[19]. You've all seen it, you know what it

---

[19] Bidder: A person who makes a price offer for an item (or lot) in an auction.

is, and we've given it a certificate of authentication. We've already got bids on the internet and I'm going to start the bidding here at… eight thousand pounds?"

Alfie grinned at Tracey and gave her a high five!

"Eight thousand five hundred… nine thousand… nine-five… ten thousand… ten-five… eleven thousand… eleven-five…" said the auctioneer as the bids came in furiously.

"This is amazing," said Tracey, and they both laughed when they looked at their parents who were sitting there open mouthed, transfixed by the bidding.

"Eleven thousand six hundred pounds... eleven-seven... eleven-eight... eleven-nine... twelve thousand pounds..." continued the auctioneer.

"I'm selling now at twelve thousand pounds...Oh! Wait a minute... we have a new bidder on the telephone... twelve thousand five hundred pounds... Any more bids now...

No… Ok it's going once… going twice… and I'm selling now to the telephone bidder at twelve thousand five hundred pounds."

The auctioneer banged down his gavel to signal the end of the auction and the whole room erupted into applause. Alfie and Tracey, their parents, and the toy expert were all dancing around the room with joy.

"We did it! We did it!" they laughed.

After the twenty percent seller's commission[20] had been taken out by the Auction House, the children received a cheque for ten thousand pounds which they gave to Alfie's dad for safekeeping while they all went out for dinner to celebrate their success.

The next day Dad took them down to the bank to deposit their cheque.

"I read about you in the paper this morning! You kids did well," said the lady in the bank to Alfie and Tracey as they paid the

---

[20] Sellers Commission: A commission paid by the seller to the auction house, which is deducted from the final hammer price.

money into their business account. "That was a lucky find."

"Well that all depends on how you look at it," replied Alfie to the lady. "We certainly were in the right place at the right time, but we weren't there by accident. And we knew what to look for when we got there because we'd studied hard and knew our stuff. We'd become experts in our niche... and we took a calculated risk[21] too. So, really, when it comes down to it, I think we made our own luck. Most successful entrepreneurs do."

And Alfie Potts was an entrepreneur!

---

[21] Calculated Risk: A risk that has been given thoughtful consideration and for which the potential costs and potential benefits have all been fully thought out.

Alfie Potts™

THE SCHOOLBOY ENTREPRENEUR

Book Four Quiz

Are you ready for Book Five in the Schoolboy Entrepreneur series?

Let's see shall we? When you've finished Book Four see if you can answer the questions below.

1. Alfie's Dad says 'the vacuum law of prosperity' means...

   a) Nature fills a vacuum... so if you want some new stuff, make a vacuum by getting rid of some old stuff.

   b) If you want new things, you should vacuum your room twice a week.

2. When Alfie and his Dad arrived at the car boot sale a man came to the car and started rummaging through their stuff before they'd had a chance to unpack. What did Dad say Alfie could learn from it?

3. How many failed experiments did Thomas Edison have on the way to discovering the electric lightbulb?

    a) 1,000

    b) 5,000

    c) 10,000

4. What are the names of the two very famous and very successful dyslexic entrepreneurs that Dad mentions?

1.

2.

5. Alfie and Tracey decided to form a 'joint venture'. Is a joint venture a…

    a) A trip to the hospital to get your granny a new hip.

    b) A temporary business partnership to carry out a particular project.

6. List 4 places Alfie and Tracey bought and sold collectible toys… (and you could too!)

1.
2.
3.
4.

7. Ralph Waldo Emerson once said …

"Nothing _____ was ever _____

without _____"

8. What is the name of the World Famous Auction House Alfie and Tracey took the truck to?

    a) Summerby's

    b) Sotheby's

    c) Christie's

The answers are at the bottom of this page. We hope you got them all right! If you didn't you'd better go back and have another read through Book Four before you move on to Book Five!

Ok, here's one more thing for you to do. Alfie and Tracey sold collectible toys, but you can sell pretty much anything at car boot sales and auctions. Can you think of 3 things a young entrepreneur like you could sell?

1.

2.

3.

If you email your car boot and auction successes to me at mark@alfiepotts.com, I'll publish them on the website, and you could win a great prize! I may even mention you in a future Alfie Potts story!

ANSWERS

1 = a; 2 = New products generate excitement; 3 = c;
4 = Richard Branson & Theo Paphitis; 5 = b;
6 = Car Boot Sales, Auctions, Collectors' Fairs, Ebay;
7 = Great, Achieved, Enthusiasm; 8 = b

ENTREPRENEURS AND DYSLEXIA

In Alfie and the Toy Hunter, Tracey mentions that she has dyslexia, and that's more common than you may think. It's estimated that 10% (and perhaps more) of the population have some kind of language based learning difficulty, with dyslexia being the most common.

Because of the way the education system currently operates, with children in year groups, and standardised testing the norm, some dyslexia sufferers may feel their self-esteem taking a bit of a blow. (Imagine seeing your school friends easily reading books and doing maths that you are finding difficult, and you'll understand what I mean).

In actual fact, dyslexia has nothing to do with intelligence, and many dyslexia sufferers are quite gifted in other areas. They are often highly creative, articulate, and inventive, with great problem solving skills, their minds seeing connections many people would not notice.

Studies have shown that up to 30% of all entrepreneurs may be dyslexic, with many saying their dyslexia has helped, rather than hindered, their business abilities!

Sir Richard Branson (who you may remember from the first Alfie Potts book) is one famous dyslexic entrepreneur who says just that…

"Strangely, I think my dyslexia has helped," he said. "When I launch a new company, I need to understand the advertising. If I can understand it, then I believe anybody can. We speak in normal language instead of using phrases that nobody understands."

And Sir Richard is not alone. In this day and age there is absolutely no reason why dyslexia should hold anyone back from success, especially success as an entrepreneur!

Here is a list of famous people from history and the modern day who were (or are) reported to be dyslexia sufferers…Why don't you google them and check out the amazing things they've done?

Leonardo Da Vinci	Albert Einstein
Johnny Depp	Alexander Graham Bell
Walt Disney	George Washington
Thomas Jefferson	John F Kennedy
Winston Churchill	Pablo Picasso
Sir Isaac Newton	Henry Ford
Sir Richard Branson	Steve Jobs
Theo Paphitis	John Lennon
Robbie Williams	Tom Cruise
Keira Knightley	Thomas Edison *(remember the light bulb?)*

THOMAS EDISON

(POSSIBLY THE WORLD'S GREATEST INVENTOR)

Thomas Edison is quite possibly the greatest inventor the world has ever seen. Here are some interesting facts about him!

Thomas Alva Edison was born on February 11th 1847, in Ohio, USA.

Thomas only went to school for 3 months! He didn't get on very well and found his mind wandering a lot. His teacher told him his mind was 'addled' (confused or mixed up).

After that his mother, an ex teacher, decided to home school Thomas hence most of his education took place at home.

He was a very curious child, and asked many questions… some of which his mother couldn't answer. To find the answers Thomas would conduct experiments. Once he tried to hatch some eggs by sitting on them ☺ and another time he accidently burned down the family barn!

To make money for his experiments Thomas went to work at the age of 12 (Wow, a schoolboy entrepreneur like Alfie!) selling newspapers and candy (sweets) on a train. He got permission to do experiments in the train's baggage car, but one day some of his chemicals spilled and the baggage car caught fire. The conductor threw Thomas and his chemicals off the train!

After this, Thomas started selling newspapers from station to station along the railroad tracks. When Thomas was about 16 he saved the life of a young boy of 3 from being struck by a train, and the boy's father, a station master, was so grateful he gave Thomas a job as a telegraph operator.

As a child Thomas suffered with lots of ear problems, and by the time he was an adult he was quite deaf. An operation could probably have helped, but Thomas refused, saying that his deafness helped him concentrate!

At age 21 Thomas moved to Boston USA and invented an electric vote recorder to record the votes in elections. It made the process faster and more accurate but no one wanted to buy it. However, in later years it was used to record votes in many States across the USA.

Thomas moved to New York when he was 22. With no money for lodgings, he slept on the floor of a basement office below Wall Street in the financial district. He spent a lot of time studying the 'Stock Market Ticker'… a machine that gave information about stock market prices. A year later he made the Edison Universal Stock Printer and sold the rights to it. Thomas expected to get $4000 for the product, but actually got $40,000!

Thomas then started his own business and later opened an 'invention factory' where he and 2 business partners could devote all their attention to inventing. The new 'factory' had around 60 people working in it and Thomas had a very entrepreneurial attitude when it came to taking on staff. He didn't mind where they'd come from or what their background was, as long as they had talent that was enough!

One particular person who worked there and had that 'talent' was Henry Ford, who went on to open his own factory... 'The Ford Motor Company'

Over his lifetime Thomas and his team went on to invent many things, some of which are listed below.

In 1928 Thomas Edison was awarded the Congressional Gold Medal by the US Congress. This is the highest civilian award in the US and is awarded to an individual who performs an outstanding deed or act of service to the security, prosperity, and national interest of the United States

At the time he received the award his work was valued by Congress at £15,599,000,000, although when he died in 1931 his estate was only valued at

$12,000,000... still a lot of money, but maybe not as much as you'd think given all his work. This is probably because many of his patents[22] had lapsed (he had 2332 worldwide) and other ideas had been pirated by competing businesses.

It's been said that Thomas Edison single handedly invented the 20th Century. That may be an exaggeration, but he certainly had a lot of influence, and many things he invented are things we use and take for granted in our lives today.

Here is a list of just some of the things invented by Thomas Edison and his team. Some of these are old so you may have to google them to see what they are, but you can imagine what an impact they must have had in their day!

1. Electric Vote Recorder
2. Fast Electric Telegraph

---

[22] Patent: A government authority assigned to an individual or organization, giving the sole right to make, use, or sell an invention.

3. Stencil Pen (predecessor to tattoo pens)
4. Phonograph
5. Improved Telephone
6. Practical Electric Lamp
7. Electric Lighting System
8. Motor that Regulates Electricity
9. Electro Magnetic Brake for trains
10. Electric Turntable for Railways
11. Electric Current Converter
12. Perforating Typewriter
13. Universal Stock Ticker
14. Electric Railway
15. Speaking Telegraph
16. Electric Locomotive
17. Kinetographic Camera
18. Rock Crusher
19. Alkaline Battery
20. Fluorescent Electric Lamp

ALFIE SAYS . . .

"I love quotes, especially those about education or inspirational ones by famous entrepreneurs! Here are a selection of my favourite quotes by Thomas Edison . . . "

I have not failed. I've just found 10,000 ways that won't work

I never perfected an invention that I did not think about in terms of the service it might give others... I find out what the world needs, then I proceed to invent.

I never pick up an item without thinking of how I might improve it.

Genius is one per cent inspiration and ninety-nine per cent perspiration.

Opportunity is missed by most people because it is dressed in overalls and looks like work.

Personally, I enjoy working about 18 hours a day. Besides the short catnaps I take each day, I average about four to five hours of sleep per night.

Our schools are not teaching students to think. It is astonishing how many young people have difficulty in putting their brains definitely and systematically to work...

Many of life's failures are experienced by people who did not realize how close they were to success when they gave up.

There are no rules here — we're trying to accomplish something!

If parents pass enthusiasm along to their children, they will leave them an estate of incalculable value.

My main purpose in life is to make enough money to create ever more inventions... The dove is my emblem... I want to save and advance human life, not destroy it... I am proud of the fact that I have never invented weapons to kill.

20577640R00045

Printed in Great Britain
by Amazon